CW00519966

Biblical Truths from a Spiritual Perspective

WORKBOOK/JOURNAL

Understanding the Concept of Inner Healing & Deliverance

Biblical Truths from a Spiritual Perspective

WORKBOOK/JOURNAL

Understanding the Concept of Inner Healing & Deliverance

Lori'Jéan Medina
&
Lion's Light International

Biblical Truths from a Spiritual Perspective, Workbook/Journal
Copyright © 2021 by Lion's Light International
First Edition: December 2021

All rights reserved. No part of this book may be reproduced or transmitted in any form or by any means without written permission of the publisher, except in brief quotes or reviews. Unless otherwise noted, all Scripture is taken from the New King James Version® (NKJV). Copyright © 1982 by Thomas Nelson. Used by permission. All rights reserved.

All definitions used in this book are taken from the Merriam-Webster online dictionary. All Hebrew/Greek definitions taken from Strong's Exhaustive Concordance of the Bible with Dictionaries of the Hebrew and Greek Words.

To order products, or for any other correspondence:

Hunter Entertainment Network
Colorado Springs, Colorado 80840
www.hunter-ent-net.com
Tel. (253) 906-2160
E-mail: contact@hunter-entertainment.com
Or reach us on Instagram at: Hunter Entertainment Network
"Offering God's Heart to a Dying World"

This book and all other Hunter Entertainment Network™ Hunter Heart Publishing™, and Hunter Heart Kids™ books are available at Christian bookstores and distributors worldwide.

Chief Editor: Deborah G. Hunter
Book cover design: Phil Coles Independent Design
Layout & logos: Exousia Marketing Group www.exousiamg.com
ISBN: 9798784825889
Printed in the United States of America.

Table of Contents

Introduction

"The Spirit of the Lord is upon Me, Because He has anointed Me to preach the gospel to the poor; He has sent Me to heal the brokenhearted, To proclaim liberty to the captives And recovery of sight to the blind, To set at liberty those who are oppressed."
Luke 4:18

This book is written out of pure necessity not because we thought it would be fun subject matter to write about. All of us involved in this book have many years of "church" in our background but have only been involved in Inner Healing and Deliverance for the last five to ten years. Our experiences vary but our heart is united in that we want to see as many people as possible set free from the bondage of the enemy. Whether that is addiction to drugs, alcohol, sex, pornography, depression, anxiety, fear, mental illness and disorders, eating disorders, or cutting, the list goes on and on. Many Christians today have been told once you receive Christ as Lord and Savior, those issues will go away and when they don't, then what? Some get frustrated, lose their faith, and walk away from God and the Church. Some just settle and think this is just the way it's going to be for the rest of their lives. That is all a lie from the pit of hell, and that is exactly where the enemy wants you. He wants you separated from God, depressed, and feeling worthless. The good news is Jesus came to set the captives free and that includes you!

Use this workbook along with the book to delve deeper into your personal, intimate time with the Lord in the process of your Inner Healing and Deliverance. This is a tool you can use alongside of your individual counseling and Inner Healing and Deliverance sessions to help you to grow stronger and more confident in your newfound freedom. Take time to pray and answer the questions from an honest and transparent place. Utilize the journaling pages to track your progress and to jot down anything you hear the Lord speaking to you. We are so very excited for your journey in Inner Healing and Deliverance, and look forward to great testimonies of God's goodness and faithfulness in your life!

Spiritual Truths & Warfare

Key Points:

1. Spiritual Warfare is real.
2. Count the costs.
3. Walk in authority.
4. Guard yourselves.
5. Understand your enemy.
6. Know the Word.
7. The battle is the Lord's, not yours.

Questions

1. What are some key things you can do daily to strengthen your understanding of spiritual warfare?

_____

_____

_____

_____

_____

2. What are some ways in which you will purpose to engage in spiritual warfare in your own life?

_____

_____

_____

_____

_____

Journal

What is Inner Healing & Deliverance

Key Points:

1. Healing and Deliverance is necessary for everyone.
2. Deliverance is often a gradual process to emotional and spiritual healing.
3. The purpose and principle of deliverance is to obtain wholeness.
4. Unforgiveness can cause the majority of pain and strongholds.
5. The Holy Spirit lives within us.
6. Remain steadfast in your pursuit of inner healing and deliverance.
7. Jesus died to set you free!

Questions

1. Who is Jesus, and who is He in your life?

_____

_____

_____

_____

_____

2. What do you feel your role is in your own Inner Healing & Deliverance?

_____

_____

_____

_____

_____

Journal

Biblical Suffering & Affliction

Key Points:

1. Enduring suffering and affliction is used as a tool used by God in our lives.
2. Suffering forces us to turn from trust from our own resources to living by faith in God's will for us.
3. We should pray for His perfect will through our suffering and affliction.
4. Suffering instructs us that God is more concerned about the individual's character than comfort.
5. Through our sufferings and afflictions, it helps us to adapt to be more in the image of Christ for our development spiritually.
6. Through our affliction, God is wanting us to stay connected with Him.
7. God wants to shine through us for people to see His mercy and grace as we journey through affliction/suffering!

Questions

1. How do you view suffering and affliction in your life?

_____
_____
_____
_____
_____

2. Are you willing to see it through the eyes of Christ and submit to His will, no matter what it looks like?

_____
_____
_____
_____
_____

Journal

Understanding Oppression & Demonization

Key Points:

1. Possession and oppression are results of unclean spirits.
2. Biblical truths make it abundantly clear that Christians can be demon oppressed.
3. As followers of Jesus, we are in battle with Satan and his evil forces, but not from within ourselves.
4. Demon possession involves a demon having absolute influence over the thoughts and/or actions of a person.
5. Some dispute that while a Christian cannot be demon possessed, a Christian can be demonized or oppressed.
6. We have the power to cast out demons.
7. "And Jesus rebuked the demon, and it came out of him; and the child was cured from that very hour."

Questions

1. Do I understand that it is God's will for me to be fully free from oppression and demonization?

_____

_____

_____

_____

_____

2. Am I willing to put in the needed time and effort to get free and stay free?

_____

_____

_____

_____

_____

Journal

_____

_____

_____

_____

_____

_____

_____

_____

_____

_____

_____

_____

_____

_____

_____

_____

_____

_____

_____

_____

_____

_____

_____

_____

_____

_____

_____

_____

_____

_____

_____

_____

_____

_____

_____

_____

_____

_____

_____

_____

Unforgiveness

Key Points:

1. Forgiveness is restoration and healing from holding onto shame, guilt, and offense in a godly way.
2. Forgiveness is an action to trust God to lead the way to righteousness and justice.
3. Learning true forgiveness is a process to let go of grudges.
4. If we hold onto unforgiveness, it becomes a stronghold for which in the long run, we will suffer.
5. When offended, we don't have to endure or take abuse.
6. We are not victims of our circumstances in the Lord.
7. In true forgiveness, it allows us to let go of the sting and pain of the offense and literally frees us from focusing on the offender to releasing it back unto God.

Questions

1. Am I willing to let go of unforgiveness and release the people that have hurt me fully to God?

_____

_____

_____

_____

_____

2. Name the people you need to forgive and release over to God?

_____

_____

_____

_____

_____

Journal

_____
_____
_____
_____
_____
_____
_____
_____
_____
_____
_____
_____
_____
_____
_____
_____
_____
_____
_____
_____
_____
_____
_____
_____
_____
_____
_____
_____
_____
_____
_____
_____
_____
_____
_____
_____
_____
_____

Resolving Spiritual Conflict

Key Points:

1. We have an adversary named Satan, who is roaming with lies, deceit, and temptation.
2. We deal with ongoing conflict, worry, tension, and stress and get stuck trying to figure out how to settle situations from out of the flesh.
3. Ask the Holy Spirit to guide you when dealing with conflict to be His voice of truth in humility and love.
4. Don't take the spirit of offense and allow unforgiveness to enter your heart and mindset.
5. The power of prayer and walking in authority shifts the conflict to reconciliation God's way.
6. The Lord wants restoration, healing, deliverance in dealing with conflict.
7. We have the power of authority in Christ to work through it all.

Questions

1. Is being right more important to me than doing right? Am I willing to lay down my desires for His?

_____
_____
_____
_____
_____

2. What can I do daily to resolve/combat spiritual conflict?

_____
_____
_____
_____
_____

Journal

Workbook Chapter 7

Anxiety, Hopelessness & Depression

Key Points:

1. The Lord wants us to live in His presence and walk in freedom.
2. It is a petition of prayer to bring expectation, faith, hopefulness, and optimism.
3. I proclaim in Jesus Christ's name to soar like an eagle by the leading of the Holy Spirit.
4. I take my authority in You and break off and release every stronghold and demonic spirit that has tried to keep me captive and in the darkness by the adversary.
5. I break off all word curses, offenses, and derogatory judgements that oppressed me into believing the lies and deception from the enemy.
6. I declare this moment to keep my eyes on You and to reflect on Your Word of Truth and promises for my life.
7. I rebuke the lies of the adversary and will no longer give him a foothold to speak into me.

Questions

1. What can I do daily to keep my heart and my mind fixed on the Truth that I am free?

_____
_____
_____
_____
_____

2. What things or people do I need to remove from my life that keep me in a state of darkness?

_____
_____
_____
_____
_____

Journal

Addictions/Eating Disorders

Key Points:

1. Eating disorders are opposing to God's will in our lives.
2. Overeating tends to substitute a lack of self-esteem and other emotional issues.
3. It is an emotional, physical, and spiritual issue.
4. As believers, we belong to God above and are made in His image.
5. We are not to surrender to the false gods of this world.
6. Our identity is in our Heavenly Father and no one else.
7. The Lord loves His children unconditionally and wants us to live for Him only.

Questions

1. How can I daily affirm myself that I am fearfully and wonderfully made?

_____

_____

_____

_____

_____

2. What things do I need to separate from that are in direct disagreement with God's thoughts of me?

_____

_____

_____

_____

_____

Journal

_____
_____
_____
_____
_____
_____
_____
_____
_____
_____
_____
_____
_____
_____
_____
_____
_____
_____
_____
_____
_____
_____
_____
_____
_____
_____
_____
_____
_____
_____
_____
_____
_____
_____
_____
_____
_____
_____
_____
_____
_____

Discerning of Spirits

Key Points:

1. Jesus extended His authority to believers.
2. Jesus gives us a picture of what intimacy looks like.
3. Intimate relationship with the Lord leads to a surrendered, spiritually sensitive believer grounded in the love of Christ.
4. The early Church recognized the impact of the demonic realm upon the believer.
5. Jesus not only discerns demonic spirits, but commands them to leave the afflicted person.
6. Prayer and fasting, in concert with the gift of spiritual discernment, are keys to effective spiritual warfare.
7. These are the hallmarks of Inner Healing and Deliverance ministry: submission to God, resisting the devil, drawing near to God, clean hands, and purified hearts, grieving over sin, and humility.

Questions

1. How can I discipline myself daily to walk in the power and authority of discerning of spirits?

_____

_____

_____

_____

_____

2. In what ways can I guard myself against deception and counterfeit spirits?

_____

_____

_____

_____

_____

Journal

The Spirit of Adversity

Key Points:

1. Adversity is used by God to draw us closer to Him for His purposes and glory.
2. Adversity reveals our weaknesses and therefore we pray the leading of the Holy Spirit to guide us through.
3. It is imperative to understand the Lord will allow us to walk through adverse challenges to grow our faith to trust Him.
4. Adversity encourages us to understand on a deeper level the grace of God.
5. If we don't armor up and battle by the strength of the Holy Spirit, the enemy has strongholds which will cause discord, fear, and spiritual oppression.
6. When we are in the midst of Spiritual Warfare, it's the battle between good versus evil.
7. "My brethren, count it all joy when you fall into various trials." James 1:2

Questions

1. Do I trust God to walk with me through adversity? If not, why?

_____

_____

_____

_____

_____

2. What can I do daily to strengthen my trust in God as I walk through adversity?

_____

_____

_____

_____

_____

Journal

The Spirit of Fear

Key Points:

1. We are to put our faith and trust in the Lord, and He shall be our refuge and strength.
2. Try to detect the fear as soon as your aware of it.
3. Write down your fears then one by one, give them to God.
4. When we worry, we are focusing on the wrong authority.
5. Just because we feel an emotion, it doesn't mean the thought behind it is true. Therefore, know the truth by God's Word.
6. Trust in God. Give Him your weakness, sadness, doubt, and fears, and receive His strength, His joy, His ability, and His confidence.
7. Remember, God has a plan for your life.

Questions

1. What am I afraid of? What things cause fear to rise up within me?

_____
_____
_____
_____
_____

2. How can I walk in the absolute peace of God?

_____
_____
_____
_____
_____

Journal

The Spirit of Offense

Key Points:

1. When offense takes root, the first place it's coming after is your way of thinking.
2. In a moment, offense attaches itself to your mind for which the ability to have clarity and peace is diminished.
3. Offense will split up our most devoted loved ones to now become a nemesis because they didn't perceive issues your way.
4. Once we get into this place of offense, it is extremely dangerous because it now attaches to your heart.
5. The enemy wants offense to destroy you.
6. Pray for those who trespass against you.
7. If the offense is not appropriately distinguished and true repentance doesn't take place, then the offense will persist to cause turmoil, confusion, disarray, and destroy relationships.

Questions

1. How can I guard myself against the spirit of offense?

_____
_____
_____
_____
_____

2. Who do I need to release in regard to the spirit of offense?

_____
_____
_____
_____
_____

Journal

The Spirit of Control & Manipulation

Key Points:

1. Spiritual control and manipulation are psychological falsifications of emotional abuse, mistreatment, and exploitation of one's emotions.
2. Manipulation and control are used for a person to gain what they want regardless of what is right or wrong.
3. Whenever someone tries to convince you to do what they want versus what you want, it is control and manipulation.
4. We are not to be co-dependent on anyone outside of the Lord.
5. Spiritual manipulation will try to control people by using their weaknesses, or vulnerabilities, against them.
6. A controlling spirit will eventually lead to manipulation.
7. Ask God to show you His truth, so that you can find freedom in Him.

Questions

1. How can I build myself up so that I am not easily controlled or manipulated?

_____

_____

_____

_____

_____

2. Who can I pray for that possesses a controlling and manipulative spirit?

_____

_____

_____

_____

_____

Journal

The Poverty Spirit

Key Points:

1. The poverty spirit seeks to crush, cheat, steal, and destroy our lives.
2. This kind of spirit attaches to a person and keeps them from relying on God, being self-reliant instead.
3. It's never enough.
4. The idolization of money is the root of all evil.
5. As believers, everything we own belongs to Jesus.
6. When man is constrained by worldly possessions, he is under the influence of the enemy.
7. When you abide in Christ, you have everything you need to live a full, rich life in the Spirit.

Questions

1. Name some ways you can cut off the Poverty Spirit in your life?

_____
_____
_____
_____
_____

2. Do you believe God wants to release blessing upon your life? How can you share that blessing?

_____
_____
_____
_____
_____

Journal

The Orphan Spirit

Key Points:

1. The Orphan Spirit is a stronghold from the enemy which causes one to feel abandonment, insecure, isolated, unaccepted, neglected, not good enough, and loneliness.
2. An Orphan Spirit can push an individual into becoming an overachiever, extremely aggressive, and competitive.
3. We are God's chosen children through His Son, Jesus.
4. If we believe in Jesus Christ as our Lord, God, and Savior, then we can be free of the Orphan Spirit.
5. If we are in disbelief of God's love for us, then the enemy has the stronghold of allowing this spirit to enter into our mindset.
6. "For you did not receive the spirit of bondage again to fear, but you received the Spirit of adoption by whom we cry out, "Abba, Father." Romans 8:15-16
7. God has loved us from the beginning of time.

Questions

1. Am I confident that my heavenly Father loves me?

_____

_____

_____

_____

_____

2. What in my childhood caused me to allow the Orphan Spirit to take a hold in my life?

_____

_____

_____

_____

_____

Journal

The Spirit of Freemasonry & Secret Societies

Key Points:

1. Freemasonry is the gatehouse to other secret organizations.
2. Freemasons are sacrilegious and believers are completely deceived if they are involved in their doctrine.
3. Freemasonry is considered by many to be a form of religion, but not of the God of the Bible and Christianity.
4. They subscribe to idolatrous, heathen, pagan, and occultic oaths, vows, customs, and doctrines.
5. "For there is nothing hidden which will not be revealed, nor has anything been kept secret but that it should come to light." Mark 4:22
6. Freemasons will take the Bible and omit God's truth to their version.
7. Renounce all claim to any connection with freemasonry and/or secret societies.

Questions

1. Who or what do I need to separate myself from in regard to freemasonry? Friends? Family?

_____

_____

_____

_____

_____

2. How can I witness to others bound in freemasonry/secret societies?

_____

_____

_____

_____

_____

Journal

The Spirit of Jezebel

Key Points:

1. Jezebel was conniving, malicious, ruthless, vengeful, and heartless.
2. People who are under this spirit worship false deities and participate in ungodly practices, corruption, manipulation, seduction, and rebellion all for the love of money, control, and power.
3. The Spirit of Jezebel is devious and scheming to manipulate and control us to go against the Word of God.
4. The Spirit of Jezebel is trying to control leaders in governments, entertainment, businesses, and churches.
5. The Jezebel spirit is a demonic spirit with no gender.
6. This spirit comes against God's morality, righteousness, and holiness.
7. Ask the Lord to expose any connection with the Jezebel spirit in your life.

Questions

1. In what ways have you noticed the Jezebel spirit operating in your life?

_____

_____

_____

_____

_____

2. Ask God to reveal any people or organizations you are connected that walk in the Jezebel spirit?

_____

_____

_____

_____

_____

Journal

The Spirit of Mammon

Key Points:

1. Mammon is a biblical name for wealth, affluence, and assets.
2. The Spirit of Mammon entices people through envy, idolization, lust, greediness, gluttony, selfishness, and materialism.
3. The Spirit of Mammon mocks the goodness of God.
4. This spirit tries to dominate you and leads you into rebellion, insubordination, disobedience, deception, swindling, misappropriation, and corruption.
5. Other indications of Mammon are determined by success and a certain standard of living which for many is living beyond one's means.
6. This spirit comes against God's morality, righteousness, and holiness.
7. The Word of God states that we cannot serve God and Mammon, because we will love one and hate the other, and be loyal to one and despise the other.

Questions

1. Do I place material things and/or personal success before God in my life? If so how?

_____

_____

_____

_____

_____

2. How can I discipline myself to guard against the Spirit of Mammon in my life?

_____

_____

_____

_____

_____

Journal

The Python Spirit

Key Points:

1. Another word for the Python spirit is *soothsaying*, which is the practice of foretelling.
2. The Python spirit represses individuals by being intrusive and preventing them from a relationship with the Lord.
3. The Python snake attacks through choking and suffocating to constrict its target.
4. The Python spirit originates back to the oracle of the Temple of Delphi, which stems back to Greek mythology in ancient times.
5. It was said that Pythia channeled divinations and prophecies from Apollo himself, while immersed in a trance like state of mind.
6. This spirit causes spiritual warfare and creates confusion and destruction in the spirit realm globally.
7. The Lord is our King and mighty ruler, and He has power and domain over all. He will cast down the wicked.

Questions

1. How do you feel the Python spirit has affected your life?

_____

_____

_____

_____

_____

2. How can I daily strengthen my walk with God to stand against the Python spirit?

_____

_____

_____

_____

_____

Journal

The Spirit of Leviathan

Key Points:

1. The Hebrew root meaning of Leviathan is "curled, coiled, entwined, and twisted."
2. Leviathan is an unclean spirit.
3. The Leviathan caused the most fearless warriors to turn away out of fear and apprehension.
4. One of the main characteristics of Leviathan is pride which hinders one from receiving the guidance of the Holy Spirit.
5. Leviathan is a calculated fighter and has a hardened heart.
6. Leviathan was used as a symbol intended for the depraved rulers of the Earth who resist the Lord's children.
7. The Leviathan spirit is: Blaming, Calculating, Conceited, Commanding, Cynical, and Deceitful.

Questions

1. Do I have pride in my life? Name what areas you may have displayed pride.

_____

_____

_____

_____

_____

2. What can I do to ensure I am not deceived by the spirit of Leviathan?

_____

_____

_____

_____

_____

Journal

_____
_____
_____
_____
_____
_____
_____
_____
_____
_____
_____
_____
_____
_____
_____
_____
_____
_____
_____
_____
_____
_____
_____
_____
_____
_____
_____
_____
_____
_____
_____
_____
_____
_____
_____
_____
_____
_____

The Spirit of Kundalini

Key Points:

1. The Kundalini Spirit derives from mysticism in Eastern religions such as Hinduism and Buddhism.
2. Kundalini Yoga teaches man that they are one in nature with spiritual divinity.
3. As followers of Jesus Christ, we are not to seek other gods, deceitful doctrines, and occultic practices.
4. When people evoke the Kundalini Spirit, it can make them do various demonic actions.
5. Several manifestations of the Kundalini Spirit are body jerking, quivering, tremors, twitching, breathing abnormally, depression/emotional issues, and force of uncontrolled energy.
6. There are several ways in which this spirit reveals itself: Meditation, Yoga, Visualization, Reincarnation, Drugs, etc.
7. Remain vigilant and watchful in these last days, so you are not deceived by false and lying signs, wonders, and miracles.

Questions

1. Have I allowed the Kundalini Spirit into my life through Yoga, Meditation, Drugs, etc.?

_____

_____

_____

_____

_____

2. What can I do to cast these spirits out of my life? How can I replace them with His Spirit?

_____

_____

_____

_____

_____

Journal

The Spirit of the Third Eye

Key Points:

1. The worldly view and purpose of opening one's "Third Eye" is not only to "Experience Higher Consciousness and a State of Enlightenment," but also to "provide insight, intuition, a clarity of vision, to reveal the truth, and provide wisdom."
2. The *witch culture* has been a steady constant through all of those things..
3. Satan operates in a myriad of ways including the natural and supernatural, philosophical, logic, science, and creation, social media, and pop culture.
4. Millennials are progressively walking away from Christianity because they were never taught about the things of the spiritual realm.
5. The world is being deceived.
6. Whether it is the Third Eye, the Evil Eye, or Witchcraft, the root of these things is power and protection.
7. We NEED the power of God!

Questions

1. Have I curiously opened my spirit up to "The Third Eye"? How can I shut the door?

_____

_____

_____

_____

_____

2. Are there people and/or things in my life that allow this spirit to operate in me, or them?

_____

_____

_____

_____

_____

Journal

The Spirit of Witchcraft

Key Points:

1. Witchcraft is enticing and conjuring of immorality and demonic spirits.
2. Witchcraft is occultic and correlates with casting spells, divination, magic, and sorcery to control and manipulate the supernatural powers for evil and greedy purposes.
3. We acknowledge there are only two sources of spiritual dominance: The Lord and Satan.
4. When we search for other knowledge, worldliness, or supremacy away from God, it is idolatry and witchcraft.
5. When practicing witchcraft, a person is entering into Satan's dominion.
6. We are protected by our spiritual armor in Christ.
7. We belong to Jesus Christ and are under His divine authority for our lives.

Questions

1. Have I dabbled in practices that opened my spirit up to witchcraft? How do I cut this off in my life?

_____

_____

_____

_____

_____

2. Where did this begin in my life? Name others that encouraged and/or participated in it. Pray for them.

_____

_____

_____

_____

_____

Journal

The Spirit of Molech (Child Sacrifice)

Key Points:

1. Molech was an ancient god worshipped by the Ammonites and Canaanites. They practiced the brutal act of child sacrifice.
2. The idol worshippers would put the children in the fiery arms of Molech and watch their children burn to death.
3. Molech is present today through abortion, the murdering of children in the womb.
4. People abort their unborn children due to being inconvenienced, selfishness, a form of birth control, and depravity.
5. "Yet your eyes and your heart are for nothing but your covetousness, for shedding innocent blood, and practicing oppression and violence." Jeremiah 22:17
6. This was a ritual sacrifice of children to a pagan deity which was an abomination to God enforced by the penalty of death.
7. Other forms of this demonic spirit is that of human trafficking, spirit cooking, and other satanic rituals involving the sacrifice of human flesh.

Questions

1. Have I participated in abortion, or encouraged someone to abort their child? Repent, and be healed.

_____

_____

_____

_____

_____

2. Do you pray for the spirit of abortion to be cut off in the Earth? Pray and seek God's face/heart.

_____

_____

_____

_____

_____

Journal

The Spirit of Pharmakeia, Spiritism & Sorcery

Key Points:

1. Pharmakeia is a form of Sorcery where people conjure up spells, black magic, and witchcraft through the help of evil spirits.
2. Pharmakeia is the abuse and addiction of drugs and alcohol, which is directly connected with sorcery.
3. When spiritists believe they have contact with the dead, they are actually in contact with evil spirits (demons) in disguise.
4. The enemy infiltrates individuals through their minds.
5. We are to guard our hearts from the adversary and the stronghold of addiction.
6. If we are believers in Christ, any form of Spiritism demoralizes one's relationship with God.
7. Sorcerers use divinations, spells, and speaking to evil spirits which is clearly denounced in God's Word.

Questions

1. Is Pharmakeia operative in my life through drugs, alcohol, or evil spirits?

_____

_____

_____

_____

2. Have I participated in any form of sorcery or spiritism? With whom? Renounce and repent.

_____

_____

_____

_____

Journal

The Spirit of Cutting, Self-Affliction & Tattooing

Key Points:

1. Cutting/Self Affliction is when individuals intentionally harm themselves. There are various names for this including self-abuse, self-harm, and self-mutilation.
2. Cutting and self-affliction is utilized to relieve hurt, sorrow, and anguish when not being able to cope with problems one must face.
3. Historically speaking, tattooing has been related to pagan practices of idolatry.
4. Pagans cut and marked their skin with the name of a false God or with an image, or symbol, glorifying some deity.
5. Self-affliction usually occurs in private and is done in a controlled or ritualistic manner that often leaves a pattern on the skin.
6. It is up to individuals to discern the motivation in all we do to glorify God.
7. "For you were bought at a price; therefore, glorify God in your body and in your spirit, which are God's." 1 Corinthians 6:20

Questions

1. Have I self-harmed, self-afflicted, or self-mutilated? Even tattoos? Write down the root cause/causes.

_____

_____

_____

_____

_____

2. How can I guard myself from cutting, self-affliction, and the addiction to tattoo my body?

_____

_____

_____

_____

_____

Journal

The Spirit of Baal

Key Points:

1. The Spirit of Baal is violent and required human sacrifice, witchcraft, cutting, and was behind all carnality, sexual sin, and perversion which is still very dominant today and intertwined with many other evil spirits.
2. These false idols and spirits usurped power and authority over those considered less fortunate, or in modern terms, the "poor of society."
3. The Lord says we cannot serve God and riches, it is an abomination to the Lord.
4. The Spirit of Baal in ranking was like a king over more inferior gods.
5. These false idols and spirits were about control, domination, and ownership.
6. The Spirit of Baal has also led people to cut their flesh when they lost a loved one.
7. Baal worship of any kind opens the door for demonic, legalistic control.

Questions

1. How do I view others in society? Around the world?

_____
_____
_____
_____
_____

2. Have I allowed a legalistic, controlling, and domineering spirit into my life? How do I expel it?

_____
_____
_____
_____
_____

Journal

Workbook Chapter *28*

The Spirit of Antichrist

Key Points:

1. Satan is in total opposition to Jesus Christ.
2. Those who acknowledge Jesus Christ came in the flesh and died for our sins and rose again are the true believers in Jesus.
3. Those who don't believe and deny Christ are followers of the Antichrist spirit.
4. The Antichrist spirit comes as a false messiah who appears to be the Christ before the 2nd coming of our Lord, Jesus Christ.
5. The Antichrist is roaming the Earth and will appear as a political leader that will create mayhem and govern the world.
6. In the end, God is the Almighty Ruler and Satan, and the demonic realm, will be completely destroyed.
7. As believers in Christ, God's Word is our hope.

Questions

1. Have I partnered in any way, shape, or form with the Antichrist spirit? Antichrist earthly agendas.

_____
_____
_____
_____
_____

2. Do you believe fully in Christ Jesus as the only way to Heaven? Explain.

_____
_____
_____
_____
_____

Journal

The Spirit of Illuminati

Key Points:

1. Illuminati is devised from secret societies such as freemasons, mysticism, and other occultic secret societies.
2. They hold their followers to underground secrecy, which is promoted by a pecking order of deity, god, goddess, idol, divine being, or hierarchy.
3. This secret society is an elite group which encompasses global power in government, entertainment, world markets, corporate businesses, and large banking institutions.
4. Their goal is to try to take over and control through world dominance.
5. They work through infiltrating the media and indoctrinating through brainwashing in ways such as subliminal messaging.
6. The Illuminati exceeds dark demonic power filtrating through power, intelligence, and wealth.
7. Many well-known organizations are a part of the Illuminati.

Questions

1. Am I a part of any organization affiliated with the Illuminati? How can I break free?

_____

_____

_____

_____

2. Am I easily persuaded through distraction and deception? How can I change this?

_____

_____

_____

_____

_____

Journal

The Spirit of Voodoo

Key Points:

1. Voodoo is a polytheistic religion with various other names which is the belief that there is more than one god, or gods.
2. Voodoo practices conjure up spirits that rule nature and include animal sacrifices, and ancestral worship of the dead.
3. Another way Voodoo is associated with spirits is through mystic dancing in which the worshippers invite the spirits to provoke them and the use of snakes.
4. There is also magical spell casting, mysterious potions/remedies, and amulets/jewelry which are charms for healing and enticing followers, while performing ungodly ritualistic ceremonies.
5. Within the utilization of Voodoo it also includes bewitchment, black magic, fortunetelling, and sorcery for evil purposes.
6. In the end, people will be held accountable for their actions in their demonic exploits of Voodoo.
7. Occultic practices of any sort are a disgrace to God.

Questions

1. Have I participated in any form of Voodoo? Explain. Repent, and ask the Lord to deliver you.

_____
_____
_____
_____
_____

2. Do I know of anyone that practices Voodoo? Pray for the Lord to deliver them.

_____
_____
_____
_____
_____

Journal

_____
_____
_____
_____
_____
_____
_____
_____
_____
_____
_____
_____
_____
_____
_____
_____
_____
_____
_____
_____
_____
_____
_____
_____
_____
_____
_____
_____
_____
_____
_____
_____
_____
_____
_____
_____
_____
_____

Yoga, Reiki & Martial Arts

Key Points:

1. Yoga, Reiki, and Martial Arts have a satanic way of programming spiritual control over our minds and bodies.
2. Yoga is a spiritual exercise which teaches how to control breathing and intended to formulate one's mind and body into harmony for spiritual transformation in one's consciousness.
3. As Christians, we are to have nothing to do with psychospiritual practices. They are demonic.
4. Reiki is performed through the palm of the person's hands to massage throughout a person's body for: relaxation, stress reduction, spiritual healing, and energy healing.
5. New Age/Reiki exists to believe that one can obtain an innate intensity of self and humanity.
6. In Eastern Asian culture, Martial Arts are highly influenced by Zen, Buddhist, and Daoism religion, philosophies, and fighting techniques.
7. Be very careful of the practices you allow yourself to connect to, not everything is beneficial to us as Believers.

Questions

1. Have I naively or ignorantly participated in Yoga, Reiki, or any form of Martial Arts? Explain.

_____

_____

_____

_____

_____

2. Have you noticed any strange things occurring in your life? Explain. The root may be these practices.

_____

_____

_____

_____

_____

Journal

Ancestral & Territorial Spirits

Key Points:

1. Ancestral spirits are spirits that come down through the generations of family lineage going all the way back to ancient times.
2. Ancestral worship interweaves sacred religious beliefs, philosophies, and practices of supplication of prayers and offerings to the spirits of the dead relatives.
3. To battle territorial spirits, we must put on our armor to war against them.
4. Ancestral spirits are often communicated with through the use of drugs, images, dreams, spells, and trances used by spirit mediums, as well as idols and false gods.
5. Ancestral spirits cannot intercede on our behalf before the Lord.
6. Familiar Spirits are found throughout the Bible in reference to evil spirits, or demons, called out by fortunetellers, mediums, palm readers, tarot card readers, sorcerers, and witches.
7. Territorial Spirits are distinguished as evil spirits/demons traveling from one location to another. They can be positioned in a geographical area. They are part of the spiritual realm to plague, taunt, and torment.

Questions

1. Have I participated in any form of ancestral worship or calling on deceased ancestors? Explain. Repent.

_____

_____

_____

_____

_____

2. Have I called on fortunetellers, mediums, palm readers, etc.? Renounce and repent.

_____

_____

_____

_____

_____

Journal

Breaking Free from Addictions

Key Points:

1. Addiction is described as compulsive, dependent, excessive lying, needy, obsession, sexual misconducts, and cravings that are out of control, illegal, and dangerous to one's being.
2. From a psychological perspective, it's defined as substance abuse drugs/alcohol, overeating, overspending, and overindulging, etc.
3. Addictive behaviors can go hand in hand with dealing with temptations.
4. With God all things are possible in making healthy choices to live for Him.
5. God's Word is encouraging and gives us the means to fight addiction.
6. Jesus came to set us free, so we must stand firm and not submit to the enemy's ploys to entrap us.
7. It's by His strength and not ours to battle against addictive manners.

Questions

1. Write out the addictions you struggle with. Ask the Lord to deliver you from them all!

_____
_____
_____
_____
_____

2. How can I guard myself from falling back into past addictions?

_____
_____
_____
_____
_____

Journal

Paganism

Key Points:

1. Pagans practice outside of the religions of Christianity, Judaism, Islam, Buddhism, and Hinduism. They worship multiple deities which are considered false idols.
2. Pagans believe that divinity and mysticism is attached and inseparable from nature, and that deity is engrained within nature.
3. Druids and Wiccans are just a couple of forms of paganistic and witchcraft practices.
4. Pagan rituals and practices were described as greedy, selfish, worldly, and materialistic, worshipping twisted possessions rather than God, the Creator of all things.
5. Paganistic rituals alter the mindset to alter states of consciousness.
6. Paganists believe they are a part of Mother Earth, and follow solar and lunar cycles in their worship.
7. Paganism is the adversary's power and deceit of the prince of this world.

Questions

1. Have I allowed paganistic beliefs to lead me in my life? Name them, then renounce them before God.

_____
_____
_____
_____
_____

2. Do I heed horoscopes or astrological signs? These are examples of paganistic worship.

_____
_____
_____
_____
_____

Journal

_____
_____
_____
_____
_____
_____
_____
_____
_____
_____
_____
_____
_____
_____
_____
_____
_____
_____
_____
_____
_____
_____
_____
_____
_____
_____
_____
_____
_____
_____
_____
_____
_____
_____
_____
_____

Satanism & Satan Ritual Abuse

Key Points:

1. Satanism is various religious or countercultural practices and movements centered on the figure of Satan, the devil, regarded in Christianity and Judaism as the embodiment of absolute evil.
2. Satanism is worshipping the supremacy of utter evil.
3. They are atheists who practice malicious, wicked, deceitful, and tyrannical rituals in the demonic realm.
4. Satan Ritual Abuse is the practice of occultic sacramental ceremonies.
5. This involves emotional and physical abuse, child sexual abuse, as well as adult sexual abuse which includes pornography, prostitution, and human sacrifices.
6. Satan Ritual Abuse is used to control, frighten, and manipulate victims to adhere to what they are told to do which in many cases, causes the person to experience DID, Dissociative Identity Disorder, formally known as Multiple Personality Disorder.
7. SRA abuse leaves the victims with post-traumatic stress, addiction issues, and crimes committed due to not processing through their experiences in a godly manner without the correct counseling/ministering.

Questions

1. Have I entertained any form of Satanism? If so, name it. Renounce and repent before the Lord.

   _____

   _____

   _____

   _____

   _____

2. Am I close to, or in a friendship/relationship with, someone that believes in Satanism? Pray for them.

   _____

   _____

   _____

   _____

   _____

Journal

Identifying Sexual Spirits/Demons

Key Points:

1. In Medieval times, these spirits came in sexual dreams and nightmares, while one was sleeping and/or real physical sexual assaults of rape and molestation through incest of family members, friends, and clergy.
2. As believers of Jesus Christ, we are cautioned against worshipping the demonic realm.
3. In the Book of Genesis, before Noah and the Flood, there were sons of God that did evil and came down and impregnated human women; therefore, resulting in giants which were called the "Nephilim."
4. Incubus is a male demonic spirit that entices men and women to forbidden sexual acts with men.
5. When a man has the incubus spirit, he is enticed into homosexual relationships.
6. Succubus is a female demonic spirit that entices sexual intercourse with a man while he sleeps, also manifesting in the form of dreaming.
7. We are to keep our eyes on Jesus who came in the flesh and died for our sins to deliver us from evil.

Questions

1. What sexual spirits/demons have I allowed into my life? Name them, and ask the Lord to deliver you.

_____

_____

_____

_____

_____

2. How many sexual partners have you had in your life? One by one, break off every soul tie with them.

_____

_____

_____

_____

_____

Journal

Spirit Guides

Key Points:

1. Spirit guides today practice New Age and Pagan beliefs and philosophies.
2. These spirit guides meditate and rely on automatic writing, centering, crystals, dream states, hypnotism, positive affirmations, and self-actualization.
3. Satan disguises himself as an angel of light, but scriptures declare that God is the Light of Truth through His Son, Jesus.
4. The Lord clearly informs us throughout His Word about seeking the spirit realm.
5. Spirit guides invoke evil spirits. These are considered *familiar spirits*.
6. Spirit guides try to encounter and elevate an intense level of consciousness, which is not of our Lord, Jesus Christ, but of the enemy's deceit.
7. It's an atrocity to be in opposition to God's will for us.

Questions

1. Have I sought the spiritual realm outside of the Word of God? Explain.

_____

_____

_____

_____

_____

2. Have I allowed spiritual darkness in my life through friendships/relationships? Name them and repent.

_____

_____

_____

_____

_____

Journal

Interjects, Astral Projection & Soul Traveling

Key Points:

1. When there are strongholds over someone, the enemy can enter the person and oppress them.

2. Interjects are detrimental to one's awareness, heart, thinking, spirit, and the essence of their soul.

3. Interjects can happen more frequently after opening your "Third Eye" because you've opened a door to a spiritual realm that anyone or anything can enter through.

4. Astral Projection is the experience (intentional or unintentional) where your conscious mind leaves your physical body and moves to a different realm (also known as an astral plane).

5. The idea is that there are multiple spiritual realms, or planes, layered on top of one another where one can experience other humans, animals, extraterrestrial beings, or places in a different time or space.

6. A demonic entity can take you to see only what they want you to believe in and see for evil purposes.

7. Soul Traveling is a term used in esotericism/abnormality to describe an intentional out-of-body experience that assumes the existence of soul or consciousness called an "astral body" that is separate from the physical body, and capable of traveling outside of it throughout the universe.

Questions

1. Have I tried to go beyond the realm of the Spirit outlined in God's Word? Explain.

_____

_____

_____

_____

_____

2. Have I sought demonic entities for anything in my life? Explain and repent.

_____

_____

_____

_____

_____

Journal

_____
_____
_____
_____
_____
_____
_____
_____
_____
_____
_____
_____
_____
_____
_____
_____
_____
_____
_____
_____
_____
_____
_____
_____
_____
_____
_____
_____
_____
_____
_____
_____
_____
_____
_____
_____
_____
_____

Familiar Spirits/Demonic Types

Key Points:

1. There are many different familiar spirits and demonic types one can be bound in.
2. Go through the list in the book in Chapter 39 and pray through and ask God to reveal.
3. If you know of anyone suffering through these familiar spirits/demonic types, walk with them in prayer.
4. If you notice any generational curses, patterns, or cycles, break them off: past, present, and future.
5. If there are others that are revealed to you not in this list, write them down and break them off.
6. Replace these spirits with the fruit of the Spirit in your life.
7. Be sure to get to the root of every spirit that has had you bound. Pull up the roots and tear down every stronghold in your life, your past generations, and your future generations.

Questions

1. Read through the different types of Familiar Spirits/Demonic Types in the book. Which pertain to you?

_____

_____

_____

_____

_____

2. Write/call them out one by one, and break them off of your life.

_____

_____

_____

_____

_____

Journal

Spiritual Perspective on Mental Disorders/Illness

Key Points:

1. Mental disorders can be genetically passed down throughout your family lineage.
2. We distinguish in mental health the spiritual realm as a believer, the psychological viewpoint, and physical issues one may be dealing with.
3. In reading God's Word, He prepares us with scriptures to rely on Him by faith for working through the emotional problems we are facing.
4. If we are not in agreement with God's Word, the enemy can cause havoc over our emotional well-being.
5. As Christians, we may be blindsided, at times, by the strongholds the adversary has over us and how it affects our mindset.
6. How we think, feel, and react to situations under the oppression can cause adverse effects over our mindset.
7. When we read the scriptures, they guide us in how to live righteously in God and rebuking the lies of the enemy.

Questions

1. Do I have mental disorders/illness in my lineage? How has this affected my life?

_____
_____
_____
_____
_____

2. How can I learn to cast off these strongholds and live a life of freedom?

_____
_____
_____
_____
_____

Journal

Taking Authority

Key Points:

1. We can surrender to God's authority by trusting, praying, and reading His Word daily.
2. It's so important to understand that the devil has power on Earth, but we have power and authority in Christ.
3. We need to learn how to be proactive and resist the enemy immediately.
4. Through the power and authority you have in Jesus Christ, you can remain fulfilled, with His peace and joy, and advance God's Kingdom work through you.
5. Authority doesn't beg, authority doesn't ask, authority commands.
6. Authority is utilized through our spoken word.
7. Authority is exercised when there is a legitimate right to utilize it.

Questions

1. Do I walk in the full power and authority Christ has given to me? If not, why?

_____
_____
_____
_____
_____

2. In what ways can I strengthen my confidence and authority in Christ?

_____
_____
_____
_____
_____

Journal

The Mind of Christ

Key Points:

1. Freedom in Inner Healing and Deliverance culminates with possessing the Mind of Christ.
2. We are made in God's image, likeness, and we bear His very nature.
3. God desires for us to dwell with Him, to make a permanent habitation in His presence and to rest in Him.
4. As we grow and mature, and receive healing and deliverance, His mind: His thoughts, His intents, and His purposes are implanted within us through Holy Spirit.
5. God's manifest glory is a direct result of possessing the Mind of Christ and walking in the power and authority given to us by our Heavenly Father.
6. Supernatural manifestations of Inner Healing and Deliverance become natural when the mind, body, and spirit have become completely yielded to the Holy Spirit.
7. To possess the Mind of Christ, ultimately, we must develop a deep level of intimacy with our Creator. We cannot have His mind without relationship

Questions

1. Do I have the Mind of Christ? If not, what can I do walk closer in intimacy with the Lord?

_____

_____

_____

_____

2. Name, one by one, the hindrances in your life that are keeping you from possessing the Mind of Christ.

_____

_____

_____

_____

Journal

From Bondage to Liberty!

Key Points:

1. In walking through the process from Bondage to Liberty, it is imperative that we ensure we are properly declaring the correct language/verbiage needed to break free from specific strongholds in our lives.
2. Jesus laid down His life for us. He was born, lived, died, resurrected, and ascended to the throne room of Heaven to free us from our sin.
3. Make confession, renunciation, and repentance a part of your daily lifestyle.
4. Walk in humility and cast down the spirit of pride in your life.
5. Declare daily to yourself who you are in Christ.
6. Gird up your loins. Facing the truth is pertinent to Inner Healing and Deliverance.
7. Pray and declare from a place and position of Victory!

Questions

1. Is there anything or anyone holding me back from absolute liberty in Christ? Name them and release.

_____

_____

_____

_____

2. What can you do daily to maintain your liberty through Inner Healing and Deliverance?

_____

_____

_____

_____

Journal

Spiritual Warfare Prayers & Scriptures

Key Points:

1. Speak God's truth over yourself in conflict and spiritual warfare.
2. When warring or praying out the enemy for ourselves without assistance from anyone else, be sure to confront the enemy, condemn the enemy, and cast out the enemy.
3. Bind and loose.
4. Remember, the enemy can hear what we say and use it against us, but he cannot read our mind.
5. Walk in faith and put fear under your feet.
6. The battle is the Lord's, not yours.
7. IT IS FINISHED!

Questions

1. How confident are you in your Inner Healing and Deliverance? Write out a prayer to the Lord.

_____

_____

_____

_____

_____

2. Who can you help today to walk in their own Inner Healing and Deliverance? List their names and pray.

_____

_____

_____

_____

_____

Journal

Other Books to Read on Your Spiritual Journey

We are so very excited as you walk along your journey to Inner Healing and Deliverance. As a ministry that has seen firsthand the wonderful fruit in our own lives in Inner Healing and Deliverance, as well as in the lives of countless individuals, we would like to recommend a few books for you to read and meditate upon. Keep these books, along with this one, close by so you will be able to reference and revisit as needed on your spiritual journey.

James L. Hanley, ThD & C Tracy Kayser, JD
Healing the Shattered Soul: Becoming the Person God Intended
(Amazon, ISBN: 978-0615678603)

Tracy Kayser and James Hanley share real life stories of deliverance from anxiety, depression, insomnia, fear, rage, obsessive compulsions, panic attacks, demonic strongholds, same sex attraction and trauma from child abuse. James clearly outlines the techniques of deliverance and inner healing that he has used to bring inner healing to those who had lost hope. James Hanley, pastor of *Moriah Bible Fellowship*, has experience in deliverance and inner healing that spans twenty years and over 5000 prayer/counseling sessions with remarkable results. Currently he takes on ten to fifteen appointments a week, teaches one or two seminars a month, and has developed a team of counselors equipped to minister and bringing freedom to spiritual captives. Tracy tells her story of deliverance from same sex attraction, isolation, depression, panic attacks, and her struggles to finally secure her freedom after years of counseling and spiritual searching. She describes her difficult journey to earn a law degree and shares the tenacious dedication to eventually secure her spiritual freedom. She no longer is drawn to same sex partnerships and is attracted and seeking heterosexual relationships, without the need to "white-knuckle" her emotions. Tracy currently enjoys a blossoming legal practice while still praying and counseling with five to ten people a week. Having received freedom she willingly desires to share with others.

Deborah G. Hunter
Holy Spirit: The Promise Left for the Believer
(Amazon, ISBN: 978-1937741518)

In an age where so much chaos and confusion has enveloped our world, where do we turn for answers? The Church is seen as the only answer, but where do we turn as Believers when even the Church is lost and confused? Jesus, as He ascended into Glory, commanded His disciples to tarry, or wait, for the Promise of another... Holy Spirit. He knew they could not witness of His Resurrection without His power, His authority, on the inside of them. Many denominations do not believe in Holy Spirit; many choose to omit these very scriptures from their teachings, but if we are to walk in the full power and authority of God in this earth, we MUST consider the full counsel of God's Word and implement it all in our daily lives. Who is Holy Spirit? What is His assignment in our lives, in the Earth? Join author Deborah G. Hunter on a miraculous journey into the purpose of the One, The Promise, left for God's people. An in-depth study that will transform your walk with God, including: 1. The Person of Holy Spirit 2. The Purpose of Holy Spirit 3. The Position of Holy Spirit 4. The Power of Holy Spirit 5. The Promise of Holy Spirit 6. The Partnership of Holy Spirit ... and Much More!

Lion's Light International exists to extend prayer and a global voice of encouragement, exhortation, and edification through instilling help, hope, healing, and the Heart of Jesus.

Our purpose is to help people walk in freedom the way the Lord has created them to! We want to show others the love of Christ by walking them through forgiveness and partnering with them to break the strongholds over their lives. Jesus set the captives free! (Luke 4:18, NKJV).

Our goal is to empower people to break free of their oppression, walk in faith, and strengthen their walk with the Lord. Ministry in inner healing and deliverance allows the Lord to move through you freely and re-center your focus on Him!

Lion's Light International (LLI) has prayed and worked with people all over the world and continues to break down barriers in people's lives daily! Our team consists of people from all walks of life who have gone through the ministry themselves. We ensure that our prayer and pastoral counseling sessions are 100% private and confidential. Lion's Light International is a 501c3 non-profit organization that runs solely based off of donations.

GIVE NOW WITH ZELLE #949-880-4941
GIVE NOW WITH VENMO @LIONSLIGHT
GIVE NOW WITH CASH APP $LIONSLIGHT
GIVE NOW WITH PAYPAL
Treasurer@lionslightinternational.org

Mail Donations to:
Lions Light International
P.O. Box 672
Trabuco Canyon, CA 92678
www.lionslightinternational.org

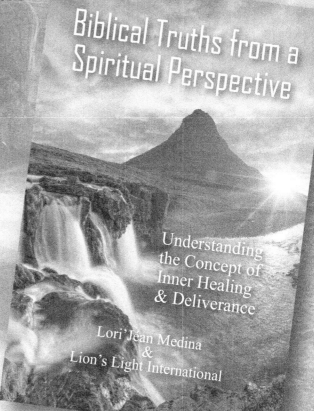

Biblical Truths from a Spiritual Perspective

Understanding the Concept of Inner Healing & Deliverance

Lori'Jean Medina
&
Lion's Light International

Lion's Light
INTERNATIONAL

Thank you for partnering with us to make the world a better place! Your donation is greatly appreciated!

Printed in Great Britain
by Amazon

26818973R00057